THE
Magdala

Your Spiritual Healing Journey

Poetically Written by Nathalie C.M. Sabbagh

Printed in Canada.

This book was created with the assistance of CanamBooks
self-publishing services

ISBN 978-1-7770487-0-9 (Softcover book)
ISBN 978-1-7770487-1-6 (Hardcover book)
ISBN 978-1-7770487-2-3 (Electronic book)
ISBN 978-1-7770487-3-0 (MOBI)

Cover and interior layout: Rodolfo Borello and Jennifer de Freitas

Cover image courtesy of:
https://www.seshell.com/tattoos/45-creative-tattoo-drawings-
for-your-inspiration/2/
Every effort has been made to locate the original artist. Whoever
you are, I thank you for your inspirational work.

Table of Contents

A Special Dedication

To Angel Rogers and the Home of Om family,
Sylvie Jutras and the Ren Xue community,
Dr. Owen Schwartz,
Maureen McRae,
Family, friends, and foes,
Shamanic tribes of the Seven Seas,
Spirit guides,
Forgotten people

...

For you were the light that guided me home.

The Mirrored Perspective

June 24, 2019

I looked at her
Deep inside barricaded eyes.
Beyond her iris'd charms,
Annual rings of growth,
Or lack thereof.
Down the rabbit's hole,
I dove.
Like Alice on the other side,
I wandered.
But …
Would I ever fall?
In love that is.
Resign the hats that drove me mad;
One day!
And yet somehow,
Somewhere,
Over the rainbow,
I dared a stare

That day.
A plunge of hued blues and decadent sins
And within her ocean's pond of wonder
A lonesome map
Left as a clue.
The place where time stands still and true
I found a door carved with a message
A secreted line before I ventured
"How I've longed for this day," it said
Marked by foreseen sight;
Perhaps.
"The key?" I whispered.
"You always had it," she said.

...

"Hush now, little Alice,
To look is to enter as one."

Prologue

The Magdala was one hell of a birthing project! Created for you is a written journey from my life's oscillated twists and turns. I call it my paradoxical, fragmented French rhapsody. The puzzle pieces that make me are the poems and tales of my inside out points of morality. The living thoughts that house my heart live in a constant state of degreed dualities. Pouring them out enables me to travel on sight, for when I write, I am the creator of life, dimensions, time, and space; the master puppeteer that strings pearls of dreams with golden clay....

Note: waltz me like you would a life sentence of never-ending tempos for such are the rhythms of music poetry!

"Get scared. It will do you good. Smoke a bit, stare blankly at some ceilings, beat your head against some walls, refuse to see some people, paint and write. Get scared some more. Allow your little mind to do nothing but function. Stay inside, go out—I don't care what you'll do; but stay scared as hell. You will never be able to experience everything. So, please, do poetical justice to your soul and simply experience yourself."
— *Albert Camus*

The Seed of Life

May 30, 2019

I am a fallen leaf from the tree of life.
They called me a seraphim when I fell from the sky.
Luckily I found my roots and learned to seed my way.
Back up the stem I went through hell to reach the light of day.

The Parable of a Woman and a Rock

May 2, 2019

There once lived a woman who sat on a rock.
She was overlooking the river.
It reflected a magical flowing piece of art.
She saw in the water a perfect standing wave.
Sitting on a throne of gliding rain she reigned.
No matter how the river preyed she stayed.
The water rock reflected her story that day:
the one about a creature hard to portray.
Inspired,
she poetted a self-portrait,
writing a story prose:
a difficult task only she could compose.
She wrote the tales of her inner sayings.
They healed her heart with rhymes of playing.
Such delights became part of her life:
a beautiful stream of enlightened sommets!

Inferno

February 12, 2019

The poisonous wise drag little vines down disgusting
debilitating annihilating knifed crowds.

The rape that takes place in claustrophobic leeched society
screeches the reaches of genuine capabilities.

The whispering penetrating tantalizing germs of dehumanizing
sperm crawling inside the cattle burns.

The silenced cries of individual flies must die for parasitic
political lies to strive.

The cultural religious abusive cuisines force feeds the genes
with obscene scenes for the killing feasts.

The brotheled debacles of cadaverous misinterpreted puzzles
are absolute nonsensical egotistical babbles.

Misery loves to breed an infectious disease spree for corruption
to breathe free.

So pray little ones.

...

Pray to the "gods" that we must serve!

The Empath and the Chrysalis

May 2, 2019

Empath is a valid word
yet my computer doesn't like it.
Asked to correct each time but I like clicking ignore.
Words have meaning
and this one means more than simple empathy.
It's feeling others to the point of losing your sense of sanity.
Being around one single person used to be extremely overwhelming.
I naturally mimicked never knowing my true self.
But
I wasn't born to walk the same way I do today.
Feeling the pains of all existence
I cried my days away.
A plague of misfortunate events took this old futile pattern.
Like a domino effect my entire life changed in an instant.
It made me embrace the word empath which healed a lifelong illness.
It wasn't mine to keep innocently imprinted from the womb.
Thirty-two years lived asleep by the nightmare of collective troubles.
Healing constructed pains with the hope to see a new light of day
was a great leap of faith.
An inner knowing that I lived the life of a dormant butterfly.
Removing layers of lies I once accepted as mine
revealed the secrets of life
beyond my chrysalis.

When Innocence Died
November 4, 2018

Darkness be bound
My Mistress is alarmed
Releasing a screaming, thundering sound
My ship's ripping sails
Her painful entrails

...

How Mistress killed sweet little nightingale!

The Lotus Tree

May 22, 2018

Did I venture too far?

Lost and blinded on purpose I'm stuck in a rut.
The forest from the trees or the woods of dark thoughts?
My thoughts like fallen leaves leave their home: a night crawl!
A crawl of mystery leads me here with cold thoughts.
Cold thoughts and memories lost in times that are brought.
Brought inside my screams I seek the dreams I've once lost.
Lost inside of me I felt creeping wounded thoughts.
Roots take hold of these and cast out the sinner thoughts.
Thoughts of miseries that were rotting in the mud.
Mud now fuels a being that has never been distraught.
A beam of energy that heals deeply-rooted thoughts.
Thoughts of new-found leaves bloom a tree with many spots.
Spots or entities and creatures that left a mark.
Victories of these this triumphant tree has fought.
Behold the lotus tree that sprung from life's downfalls!
It shines translucently with the strength of waterfalls.

Breathe

May 18, 2018

What happened to me when I drowned in pure love?
Where no raw deals surfaced buoyantly in sight?
There floated existence, so happy to be
I befriended her and she adopted me.

...

Now my heart craves her beautiful waves of reciprocity.

Hollowed Space

December 1, 2019

What should I do when unconditionality becomes my rule and
I've outgrown the mortals?

When I've long passed insurmountable paths of rubble?

I wonder what will be when one won't cower away or fail
to see what follows.

Arise Lorelei!

Smile with the guise of the devil!

For in this truffled wallow

lies a dormant rebel

and we shall bask in the stillness of hollows.

My Dearest Crow

December 12, 2017

A night of random intertwined paths
Hypnotic eyes tamed Medusa's wrath
A crow at heart beneath the man
He wore a soul not of this land.

My dearest crow, how bold is he?
To look where others dare not see
Between the realms true kingdom be
Disguisedly perched by a nightly sea.

My dearest crow, I must thank you
For in my passings I met you
A slivering road the colour of gold
Was seeking treasures of stories untold.

Just a Thought

April 1, 2019

My dearest Beau,

I must confess that I, in fact, see one flaw in life. Perhaps one mistake that I would rectify should the Gods grant me all powers of grace. I would forever erase the format in which we humans have chosen to communicate. I look at language and how it fails us each time lips part to let out a thing called a 'word' to so arrogantly describe essences beyond someone else's concocted order of letters. Yes; I can play with words or toss them aside. I can summon poetry and depict love in every which way that I want as I cry out: "You are the universe to my soul where my inexistence is cured!" But to what end and with what cause? It leaves me sad and distraught in thinking: "Is this really the best way to connect our hearts?" Language will never encompass the millions of constellated thoughts that come and go out for a walk. How could it ever when thoughts travel faster than words and words are left to summarize a world full of wonders? When punctuation and grammar dictate a rhythm that can't be constructed? I see God when our eyes connect! Where for a split second there is no time nor place but a pocket in space where we both reside in bliss. Yet as soon as that second passes I am left long forgotten from the moment that was shared, for words come to destroy an entire life that was exchanged in absolute silence....

Love,

Sweet Nothings

Merkabah

April 14, 2018

My fellow friends, dim the lights down low
For I am inspired by the mood of the flow
It calls to me like a moth to a flame
My eyes are drawn by the lines of her frame
I heard she holds knowledge of the worlds
Holding her would provoke a surge of love words

Oh Merkabah! My sweet Merkabah!

Will you put out?
You and me baby on a night out?
I'll seek out things that you didn't know
For you, my love, I'll put on a show
My sweet unspoken language
Experienced in different stages
Your sacred symmetry... I'll use through the ages

Oh Merkabah! My sweet Merkabah!

Twenty-four faces trapped in your sea
Eight pointed truths you're hiding from me
Four elements you've combined subtly
The power of three repeated constantly
Two sacred bodies intertwined within
One act of creation I felt through your skin

Oh Merkabah! My sweet Merkabah!

Finding your heart's the Mecca I seek

Tomorrow

February 3, 2019

Tomorrow,
Tomorrow …
Tomorrow never came.
Waiting for tomorrow …
Passion died in vain.
The Eve of tomorrow
Was branded as a game
Marked down upon her children
Forced out to sit and wait....

Tomorrow,
Tomorrow …
Tomorrow once again!
For the promise of tomorrow
Shall never be obtained
Enslaved to a petty garden
Raped for personal gain
Used for a pretty penny
Or treated like a snake.

So tomorrow,
Tomorrow ...
Tomorrow's turn to wait!
The Eve of tomorrow
Grounded in today
Sent from the Palace of Justice
Voice of the modern way
Speech from the Adam's apple
Will dialogue among equals at play.

Midnight Jack

April 22, 2018

A breakdown of events in point form:

Picture a pitch black night in a misty room of sassy jazz.
There she stands....
She is a lady of the mike blinded by the bright shiny lights.
The place is packed!
She sees no one.
She only senses shadows that chatter away with a clickety-clack.
Cigar and cigarette perfume consumes her lungs.
She inhales slowly ... deeply.
She looks around.
She parts her lips.
She pauses....
She sets the tone.
She's experienced in the art of seduction.
She lures them all.
Great men take notice.
They're intrigued by her "je ne sais quoi."
But these are also pompous men with reserved judgements in their hearts.
She likes to tease as her lips pull back into a smirk.
She sings the blues of repressed desires.
She does it well.
She does it raw.
She does it with a hint of pizzazz all night long.
This makes her good money:

"Let them think that they've got me, honey!"
Her shift is over.
She's bored....

She's so bored!
It's the same game all over again:
A man will approach her tonight.
He always does!
Only one mystery remains:

"Which one this time around?"

Exhibit A:

The man who puts her on a pedestal.
That man knows nothing of himself!
That man wants to pretend play.
That man comes in with a perfect escape plan.
That's a look she sees.
That's a look she knows.
That's a look that smells.
That's a look that reeks of desperation!

Exhibit B:

The man who breaks her spirit.
That man hates himself!
That man wants to be dazzling in her eyes.
That man knows how to put her down.
That's a look she sees.
That's a look she knows.
That's a look that smells.
That's a look that reeks of condescension!

The door opens....
A different specimen walks in.

He was the bringer of rain.
He was the bringer of change.
He had a reputation for chaos.
He had a reputation for getting ladies lost.
His name was Midnight Jack.
She snaps at him:

"Hit the road Jack!"

He doesn't flinch:

"Not tonight sweetie!"

They stare at each other.
A staring contest.
A perfect standoff.
A perfect standstill.
She changes her stance.
She stands still.
She calms her breath.
She channels the wild.
She has predatory eyes.
She longs for this.
She knows much of mayhem.
She was born and raised by it.
She doesn't break eye contact.
She waits patiently.
She waits for her perfect timing.
She waits for the perfect time to strike.

He yells:

"Hit me!"

She whispers:

"No!"

She catches him in a hug.
He is taken aback.

"Why would you do that?"

"Because the best pleasures in life come with shackles and the high you get from learning the sleight of hand that breaks you free."

"How do you break free?"

"By complete surrender!"

He looks at her:
That's a look she sees.
That's a look she knows.
That's a look that loves.
That's a look that she knows how to embrace.

Moments in Time

October 01, 2018

If I lived inside my grandfather's clock
I'd repurpose the timber and build a great dock
I'd walk to it each day the seconds flew my way
See an arrow tick away every minute of my stay
I'd leave worries behind with a kiss for goodbye
Watch Time's Oceanic Bay embrace tears of Yesterday
I'd befriend this old dome
Turn it back to a home
There I'd churn my wild thoughts now set free, young at heart
I'd forgive, forget, reset, and restart
Watching mister Time lose track and freak out
I'd play hide and go seek with the infamous Week
Go out prancing for no reason each time Time would change
the season
I would partner and dance with loose parts made in France
They would show me the world as the hours would turn
I would spin counterclockwise recreating balanced lifestyles
Showing all that I know to this Land of Unknowns
Lastly stated on my list is a moment not to miss
For I'd fall in love with King Infinity if Time himself would show his
true face to me

Monkey No More

November 23, 2018

Dance, monkey, dance!
Claps the hands of your Gods
Looking down for entertainment
We are unattached and bored.
Little ants down below!
Little creatures without souls!
Unaware tools of no importance
We shall use and leave to roam.

Who are you to guide or control?
Your crushing hand is unbearable:
I suffocate from its "loving" embrace and yet I claim to call it home.
How did the path to enlightenment become a never-ending winding road?
Trauma and release....
Trauma and release some more....

Regress in self-worth for your true self to come forth.
Spin around, lift off, and surrender without pause.
Breathe quickly my dear....
We are not done by far....

You're me!
I'm you!
I'm not?
Oh no....
No more!
I'm done!

You're not!
Here's more:
Be present little monkey but work for a goal.
See your own silly future be left at the door.
Dance, monkey, dance!
Work hard for your coal!

The little engine that could is broken once more....

Repair, repeat, cry out and roar!

These musical fields are acoustically poor!

Change, upgrade, and look back no more for this life has beauty, trust us we're sure.
Ascend but stay grounded!

Oh Masters ... I'm sore!

Master omnipresence to soar once more.
Experience!

Withdraw!

Come back this isn't the last straw!
Breathe ...
Look out!

A bird?
A plane?

Nope ...
It's trauma once again.

Know what you want!
Voice it aloud!

[...]

Don't expect a thing for your head's in the clouds!

Monkey sees!
Monkey wants!

Bad monkey ...
Attachments were not taught!
What does monkey want?
Just ask to get!

[...]

Silly little monkey, for only we know what's best!

Monkey won't play.
Monkey gives up.

Come back little monkey the game is not done!
Banana for monkey will make it come back.

Monkey is better with good thoughts on track.

Oh little one your mind has come undone
Thoughts are for observing ...
Be still and move on.

Chaotic Prose

October 22, 2018

Beautiful nonsense opened up her sight
Wishing bells' commander of hypnotic nights
The meaning of this life a true chaotic prose
The musical delight of dreaming for a rose
A simple complex essence tormenting my insides
It would not could not slumber to all poetic trials
This wordplay without form that could not be described
It led me to a door so beautifully disguised
The perfect side of chaos: a spiral not a line
A universal comeback of losses that are lies
Hope had dreamt of death trapped inside a box
Weeping wonders lost to Pandora's thoughts
The making of a note harmoniously inclined
Birthing rhythmic music: a sound no longer blind

Love Poetry

March 5, 2018

"May you bear witness to this poetry

A love so great that laid dormant in me

No longer blind

I set you free

You are enough, always, and forever will be."

Would you ever dare? Write yourself love poetry? I've done it for others once, twice, or maybe thrice. Perhaps considered taboo in this society, an illusion of narcissism that taints an otherwise natural chemistry. Today I've decided to hold a space of love within me and invite all to compose their own eclectic symphony. Let it give you the courage and strength to do the same with a daring vulnerability....

... And so it is!

To the mothering child that grew from within,

I've been your own mother for far too long and walking alongside you I couldn't go on. I've seen you cry in utter silence to render yourself invisible to everyone else. The hardest things I've ever seen you do: to others, no ... that would never be you.

You've put yourself down over and over. How could you? Numbed and believed cursed, I patiently waited to embrace you.

My baby, it's me! You don't need anyone else. For what's stronger than nurture, care, and love for oneself? You had to experience and learn from life's mess. There's no such thing as a bad darkness: without it you would've never craved the best.

Thank you

To the warring peace-maker that conquered her fears,

Words cannot express the strength that you possess: a warrior of your time without a proper quest. For decades you carried others' burdens inside: it slowly broke your body but never your pride.

Your kindness is strength but should never turn you blind. Precious to realize that these old ways must die. Death can go back to rest in the devil's eyes. Your self-loathing has no bearing. Enough! Move aside! A second of love can move mountains within. I'm forever grateful to see beauty inside my own demise.

Thank you

To the loving beloved reflecting all that is healed,

Innocent and so naïve! Built by society and culture: "Who couldn't have foreseen the misery?" Led to believe you were weakly incomplete bound to spitten vows of false poetry.

Love out of need won't satisfy me for it's based on fear of what's missing, you see. But I'm not lacking so why should you be? My love is unconditional, pure, wild, and free. Don't ever convince yourself otherwise, your light emanates from me.

Thank you

Finally, to the blossoming love that wished upon a dream, your one completed symmetric being has found infinity.

From Dawn to Dusk

March 31, 2018

I lie over the grass and look up at the stars. I know that the
greatest love story ever told is the one right before my eyes.
As I begin to write this story I have yet to know what it will be:
a tragedy like that of Romeo and Juliet or a simple comedy?
Appropriate at first glance yet they share a secret between
themselves. My Moon Goddess and Sun God, I see your whispers
fall down! They pour inside me from dawn to dusk. I breathe in
awe for the scent is a beautiful sight.

Yesterday I assumed that these two were cursed. Day in and
night out never to be together for one must govern the day
while the other rules the night.

Slaves to the cosmic law of balance with no place to go but
round and round again.

One always approaches yet the other pulls away. Left to wonder
why she runs while in her eyes he does it too in the same way.

On Earth, they have been told to look away.
How he brings them light and power yet ... they still look away.
He feels good on their skin but it burns if they stay.
Shining so bright that others naturally gravitate.
Yet he radiates alone; why?
Is it a price to pay?

As for her, she is hurt by the superstitious. Beware of her
fullness!
"She brings out deadly creatures," they say.
Why must she be the bigger person inside?

Her compassion is innocent but put to the trial. She receives only pain: the chaotic side of things.

These are forgotten children most wounded within.

But today ... Today feels brighter!

My perspective has changed.

I do not curse them for together they reign.

A love she will forever invite: an image so far-fetched to her yet never out of sight.

They are never apart; just look at the skies.

How together they stand each sunset and sunrise. Always reaching to her even through space. Don't be fooled by Earthly touches, there is always a space!

His love for her keeps him ignited.

It's a fire, a phoenix, a love that consumes and fuels him within.

He honours her space: she's in joy so beaming!

How he watches her dance and twirl around the Earth ... it's her sacred rhythm.

She's the midnight sun that rises in her domain.

You would tear her apart yet she flourishes there.

So do a million plants and creatures for whom she truly cares.

A Forgotten Journey

2002-2020

It was a beautiful day!

The sky dome had opened its windows letting light shine through the clouds.

The warm wind felt like such delicate silk wrapped around my body.

The sweetness of Spring was invading my senses.

Who would have thought the distinct smell of mud to be so insightful?

I was at the very base of a tree overlooking a woman sitting by the sea.

She seemed so peaceful mounted on a rock.

Ah ... The act of observation without thought!

I felt crushed by society offering me no time for such pleasures.

The birds would chirp as the butterflies fluttered.

The leaves of trees grew to protect blooming flowers.

Mother Nature had birthed a new cycle of life in my presence ... and it was good!

The act of observation soon turned into rumination.

The escape was impossible for I could not teach my mind to stop being rational.

It would be like asking the conscious to understand the unconscious.

Actively or passively one always thinks!

During the day as one breathes or at night as one dreams.

I think therefore I must be a rational beast!

I had separated a flower from harmony wondering when it would lose its beauty.

Inhaling the last breath of the red rose perfumed my mind with thoughts galore.

"What is the meaning of my life?" I asked.

"Where do I come from?"

"Was I already predestined to do something?"

The list went on until tears rolled off my face.

They shook the grass upon the wrath of their embrace now forming an auspicious-looking older woman.

My body got struck with all kinds of emotions.

In Awe I bowed down and cried out:

"Are you the all-knowing one?"

"No," replied the elder. "I am but the mirror of her and my purpose is to help you seek the answers to your questions. This is why you must journey west past the mountains where you will find an enchanting river. Sit at the top of a rock near the fallen tree and wait until She appears.

You must go now and good luck!"

While wanting to thank her, she vanished and I embarked on my journey.

I ran through the wind branches scratching down my spine.

Years had passed and I had changed yet even in trying I would not quit.

Tired, I took the scenic route and for a moment I thought I could retire but pleasurable things would no longer matter, for I was one step closer to what surely was the enchanting river.

What an appropriate name!

Its waters were of a fresh turquoise that shimmered the souls who dared to look upon it because it was beautiful!

I sat down to absorb the view losing myself to an old forgotten journey.

What a moment!

I cried and cried for a little while.

So much time had gone by but I had discovered who I was.

The time spent along this quest was nothing short of a fantasy.

I looked in the water surprised to see the enchanting river reflecting the elder in me.

L'Eau de Vie

Sept 6, 2019

The echoing verving urge;

the waterworks when floods converge.

Vibrations!
Undam dry siege!

Reverberate one pulsing being!

A sway to moonlight,

a floating boat,

the push and pull between sacral notes,

the tides,
the follies,
Eau de free speech!

One bedspread with jewels of thieves!

A knighted brall, euphoric scent,
a sired song, a transic chant,

thy kraken's gift laced with a bow,

exuberates my awakened bowl.

La Madeleine

June 23, 2019

I leave you with the mirage

You chased alone for years

It promised you eternal love:

An Oasis Prophecy.

So my darling mirrored image

You have returned to me

I am your written Shangri La

...

Your book of poetry!

P.S. Dance, sing, write, O frolic! Bow in a still stance from a single string this puppet shall say, "How you were the puppeteer that held me with no strings my entire play!"

Fin

About the Author

I Am

January 18, 2019

In the beginning of time I Am was but a void
Trapped by its own confusion: a blank slate of nothing more
Alone, bored, and used as a beacon.
It shined for what? A meaningless reason?
I Am felt useless and cursed by the dark
What but a need to travel when I Am thought out an ark?
Surrendering the nuisance of soundless sleepless nights
It then created oceans by crying tears of life.
What's this to its dismay? An echoing surprise!
A distant spark of hope reflecting I Am's eyes.
It sighed, no longer dull; a foreign sight so bright
I Am found inner purpose: no more nightmares tonight!
I Am went out to voyage beyond the tides of space
Reaching nebulas of time; experiencing what is.
Upon returning home I Am chose the wrong way
Trapped in a sea of glass; where is I Am today?
Swimming against reflections of illusionary states
It took I Am a while … eternity some say
It found the missing pieces to walk out of a maze
I Am learned a great lesson; one that was long craved.
Inspired to make mirrors showing true light of grace
I Am would share the love, wanting to be embraced
So when I Am forgets the state of its own face
It simply looks at you for who Am I today?

Epilogue

Long before the written word was the art of storytelling,
storytellers were responsible for passing along tribal wisdom
from one generation to the next. I walk among those whom
have been called to speak from the heart. May these words bring
forth the light as I grow into this sacred and ancient knowledge.
My name is Nathalie and this was "my" healing journey.
I Am is now complete.

('My Little Gaina' is the only poem that was left in its original
innocent state. It's a reminder of where I've started
and how much I've grown)

My Little Gaiana

December 25th, 2017

If Mother Gaia could speak in ways that only your heart
could hear;
Do you think she would cry and scream from bleeding ears?
Every day she feels the chemicals penetrating her veins.
Every day the life she shelters is slowly taken in vain.
Would she blacken her heart from the wars she must support?
Or bear the stomps and rattles of humans building forts?

"Today most have forgotten about me.
How my strength is greater than one tree.
I will always be sacred, you cannot know;
The things I have seen, done, or show.

To my little Gaiana what can I say?
You who feels me the most every day.
You will forever be sacred to me;
For you are my blood, my vein, my seed.

I will not die, Gaiana, and neither will you.
For you are me and I am you.
So run in our forests, fields, and lakes.
Breathe for me what is clean and cast away the fake.
Child of me born shackles free;
You will show others our sovereignty.

And if you ever feel weak, abused, or possessed;
I will show you a flower born out of stress.
That flower is you, Gaiana, can't you see?
My princess, my queen, you will always heal me!"

New Earth

October 3rd, 2019

Find me in the new world where my ancestral twirls have long
burned, for they've learned to phoenix yearn and run barefoot
free flowing for all who dare swim in deep knowings where all
unknown paths that I seek carve out Ceasarean roads to roam
tongue tied "Jolie" my shackles freed.

...

So it is,

And it is done!

Forever my feathers,

Ouroboros chimes,

Sway to my precious lullaby rhymes.

The wheel of karma is a trapped mind lost within the maya
of tragic times.

...

No more my Gaianas!

No more!

Let the old everlastingly rest in peace.

Give back what no longer belongs to your fields.

Forgive those who didn't know any better.

Know that they did the best with what they were taught
mattered.

...

Reach for the stars and the glistening.

Be one with all but seek within.

For in the whispers

Love's abiding.